A Wrap Dress

Katie Ashlyn Collins

BookLeaf Publishing

India | USA | UK

Presentation by *BookLeaf Publishing*

Web: www.bookleafpub.com

E-mail: info@bookleafpub.com

ISBN: 9789360942533

First edition 2024

To Little Bear, the mighty

ACKNOWLEDGEMENT

With thanks to my family and all of the friends that have helped as readers.

PREFACE

Dear Reader,
Hello! Welcome to my book of poetry. I hope you have a good read.
Sincerely,
Katie Ashlyn Collins

SECTION I

Insecurity

A Wrap Dress

I am a wrap dress—one tug away from coming undone.
The pretty façade barely covers the intimate parts
The parts that I don't want the world to see.
The parts that spill over the edges of hemlines and necklines
As the mess that I am expands and explodes
Beyond anything a seamstress could ever account for.
And there is no time to find a new façade—
A bigger, roomier one—
Because I spent my whole life crafting this one.

Everything someone says or does,
It feels like they touch on the ties holding me
together
And I'm living in fear of the day when someone
actually pulls
And I fall apart.
Because there are some things, I don't want the
world to see.
I don't want the world to see me scream or cry
Like a child in a tantrum
And write off my pain as a self-involved
delusion.
I don't want the world to see me break
Like the camel with that last straw
And assume that I'm freaking out over nothing
Because it was really a million things stacked up
that finally made me break.
But most of all,
I don't want them to see me slowly unravel
Like a frayed ribbon yanked apart by an
impatient little girl.
Because I'm scared that the mess that I am is all
that I'll ever be.

Burnt Popcorn

Independence is the burnt popcorn that I microwaved for a minute too long when I was six years old.

But I kind of liked the taste.

It's the empty wall where I can hang whatever I want–even if I regret it all when I spackle over the holes before the end of my lease.

It's the grocery cart that only I get to fill–even if I'll throw half the vegetables out in a week because I was never going to eat them.

It's the heels I wore to a twelve-hour shift–the blisters, yes, but also the compliments.

When I got older, I began to make popcorn on the stove top.

And when I make a batch that's just for me, I'll let the last popcorn sit for just a little too long.

When I smell the smoke, I know I've done it right.

I still like the taste.

Head on Collision

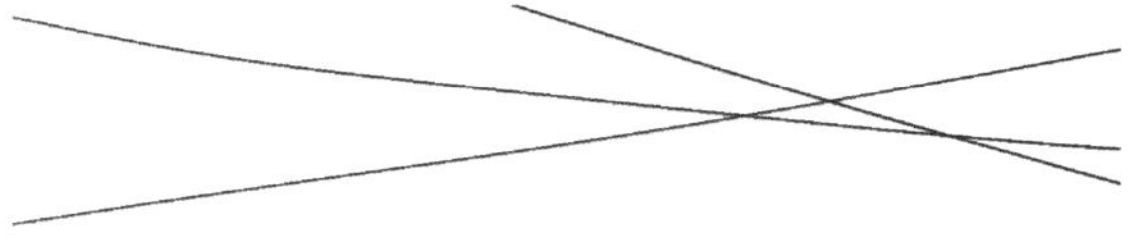

I could have died
>and all I can think is
>>'The light was green. Wasn't it?'
I tell my mom and she tells everyone.
>My uncle says not to change lanes
>>when you're at an intersection.
An eighteen wheeler took a left turn
>Right in front of me
>>and the only focus
>>was on how I could have prevented it.
As if a five-four woman can stop an eighteen
wheeler in its tracks with a hand signal.

But the scariest thing
        is the knowledge that you
                can do everything right
                        and it may not matter.
Because an eighteen wheeler took a wrong turn
and it stopped me in my tracks.

Illusion

I'm no taller than you in the morning
It's hard getting dressed when you're smaller
than your shoes
It's a thing to which I'm used
So I soldier on
My own frame is a small and a frail one
Shoulder pads give me strength that I always
wanted
I grab my power and flaunt it
It's illusion

Driving

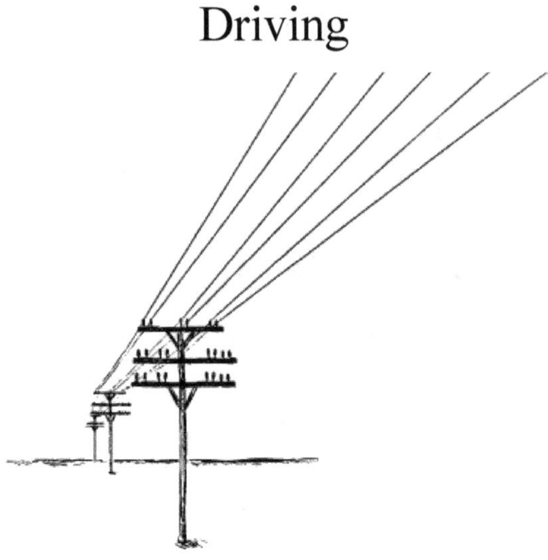

Thirteen hours pass slowly when you're stuck behind the wheel.
I have almost everything I own in the backseat of my car.
I guess you can go home again.
A half a box of Krispy Kreme is sitting to my right.
I tell myself I won't have another one, but there's another three hours to go.
The traffic jams may slow me down, but at least they let me rest.
The only reason I do these drives is to limit the days I spend like this.
I always feel so trapped by the time I won't be getting back.

Change

I used to kiss the poster on my wall
And dream of becoming Mary Kate Olsen
My days were filled with watermelon lip gloss
and climbing trees
I used to kiss boys and dream of becoming Alice
Hale
My days were filled with glittery vampires and
notes in the margins
I think of kissing you and dream of being an
obscure 18th-century playwright
My days are filled with heatless curlers and the
low pressure light I've been ignoring
And yet I wonder if my life is changing once
again

Dressing Room

I've never seen so many mirrors
Yet so little of myself
I'm hidden in the costumes and the stage
make-up
Maybe there's a little something in my eyes
Behind the tiredness
They say you put yourself into everything you
do
I must have so little self left if this is all I have to
give

Adventures of a Wacky Side Character

I'm wearing a dress made of markers.
I'm driving a kayak down the street.
I'm making the folks at home laugh while you
carry the weight each week.
Growth is beyond me.
I'm not here to grow.
I'm here for your entertainment.
And for your education.
I'm the person you shouldn't be.
I'm too loud.
Too bright.
Too colorful.
And so I live in the B-Plots.

Showtime

Do you know the feeling you have when you
hear your voice in a recording?
Imagine that amplified by the actors speaking
the lines that you dreamed up last night or,
worse, the ones that you stole from your own
life?
Because it hurt enough the first time I heard it,
But it doesn't feel real anymore.
And the ephemeral fades into memory and I tell
myself each of my characters were the only ones
to feel anything.
I'm above it all.
Until I'm not.
And when I'm not, I take notes because what am
I if not productive?
Somehow seeing another person live my life
makes everything alright.
I'm dissociating.

Vault

My emotions are under strict lock and key
Does anyone know the password?
Don't look at me.
I've never been good at understanding myself.
I've only figured it out by the process of
elimination.

Shadows

My hair feels heavy.
As I sit here, it drags me down.
There's something strange about being stared at.
But it's easier to focus on my hair than their
eyes.
The artists study me.
They see Mona Lisa.
I see empty frames in the corner as they each
outline my brow.
'Be sure to catch the shadow'
And I look to the right ever so slightly to capture
that shadow–ignoring the shadows within.
I look at the same thing in the corner.
An old weathered door knob–unattached.

The practical made impractical.
The doorknob has a man's face and metal arms
that beat on its own fat, metal stomach.
It rests on an empty birdcage.
The artists find beauty in these useless objects.
I wonder if I am one of them.
I curl and uncurl my toes.
It's the only movement I'm allowed.
Others record who I am.
How I am.
What I am.
And nothing I do or say remains–
Only my image.
And so my image becomes a shadow of the
person I once was.

Formidable

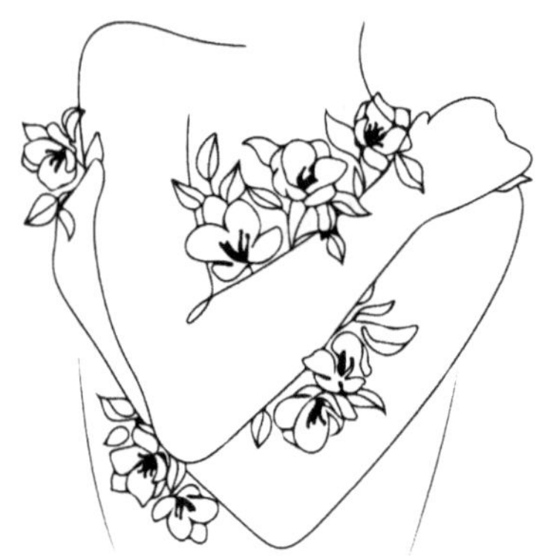

Intimidating.
You find me intimidating.
I can bake cookies by the dozen.
Braid hair.
Cover shifts.
Bend over backwards to be kind.
And I will still be intimidating.
Because softening my voice and biting my
tongue can only hide so much.
Just standing near me, you feel everything.
You feel the shaking at my core when the wrong
thing is said or done.
You feel the judgment I won't voice to make
things easier.
You feel me just beneath the surface.
I must be formidable.

Overbearing

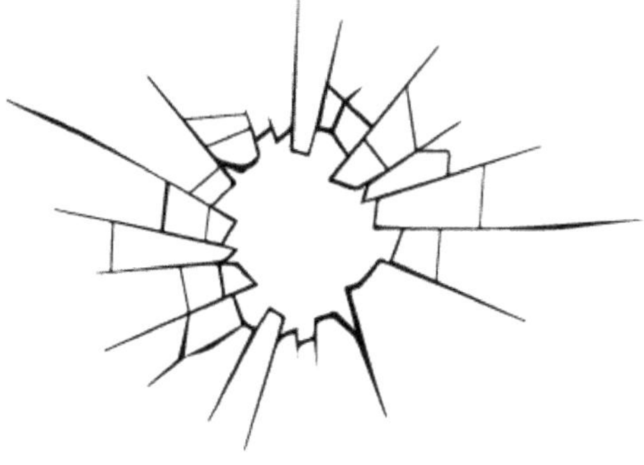

In the mirror, she sees a princess—dainty, regal, soft.
When she hears herself speak, every other word is sugar.
When she touches her skin, it's all lavender and lovely.
But if that's who she is...
Then why are the villagers running?
Why is the town on fire?
Why is the ground shaking with her every step?
Poor Girl.
There's no such thing as a dainty dragon.

SECTION II

Anxiety

Waterfalls

The waterfall is beautiful
But living under it created too much pressure.
I kept trying to push through and make my way
beneath the curtain
But the current's too strong.
I won't let myself drown.
Sometimes I imagine a world where I kept
pushing.
I imagine imploding under a waterfall must be
beautiful
Like I'd implode into a mess of wildflowers
flowing down the river—
Beautiful;
Tragic.

Instead, I walked around, swallowing my
melancholy, and I found another way beneath
the curtain.
One that didn't destroy me.
I wasn't impaled into roses, but my heart still
beats.
That has to be some kind of beautiful.

The Cut

I sleep with scissors on my bed
I don't know when it started
I would never have actively chosen to sleep with
scissors on my bed
You see, I move a lot in my sleep
Putting teddy bears in headlocks was a common
occurrence
So I wouldn't have chosen this
But some forgotten night I must've worked too
late and too long and fallen asleep mid-project
With the scissors in my bed
And for one night, I slept peacefully
I did not toss. I did not turn. I did not move.
Why? I don't know.
Maybe I was tired. Maybe I was scared.
I know I slept well that night.
And now I sleep with scissors on my bed.

Passed Out

I should have eaten more today.
Or eaten protein at least.
A half a sleeve of oreos is hardly a feast.
But time, it got away from me.
I focus on my work to my own detriment.
I'm typing each and every word I write in
cement.
I want it to last so some silly girl can go through
the stacks in a library one day and fall in love
with who I was.
I have to believe, as a memory, I'm easier to
love.
I have to believe the work I do will matter to
someone.
I wake up on the floor with people gathered
around.

Chaos

I like clean-cut. Order. Planning.
Smooth lines and clear boundaries.
Easy. Sane.
It makes everything work.
Until the unexpected brings in chaos.
And while I like clean-cut, I love chaos.
Even as it crushes my careful plans, there is
something in the flurry of insanity that sparks
when everything goes awry.
When boots hit the ground.
Because chaos shows you who you are.

Mistakes

I wish I saw each backstep as one brief
intermission.
As if the world would go back to the same place
I left behind before I broke the balance.
Each character is back in the same place they
were before the curtain closed.
I could use fifteen minutes to go to the bathroom
and cry in private
Or scream inside my car.
Anything that would keep me from showing
who I really am to anyone else.
Because no one's perfect, but don't we all want
to be?
Maybe that's just me.

Wildflowers

In my dreams, we ran from a tornado.
We ran through a field of flowers thinking,
'Surely, it can't destroy something this
beautiful.'
But it kept coming.
So we ran through the field of flowers
We jumped into a far-off meadow
And as we landed, I looked back.
When I saw the flowers violently swirling
around the air,
I thought 'What a lovely destruction.'
I almost wanted to join them.
But then I looked back at the field where they
once were–now barren, broken.
Torn apart without a root left for next season's
bloom.
One lovely moment is not worth the desolation it
leaves in its wake.

Echoes

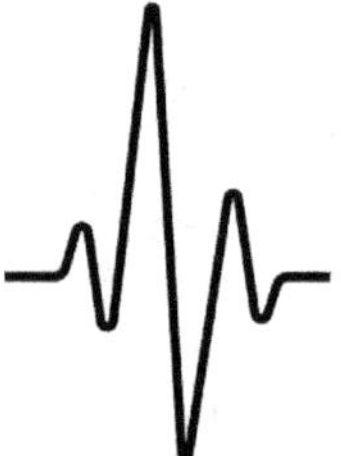

I thought the click-clack of my heels were the
trumpets announcing the arrival of the force I
imagined myself to be, but as I got older, their
echo sounded more and more hollow.
Click. Clack.
Can you hear me?
Do I need to hire a trumpeter?
And will that be enough for me?
Will blowing into party favors everytime I enter
a room make me matter?

Afterthoughts

The phone calls I couldn't return.
The trash I didn't take out.
The vitamins I never take.
I don't just want to be better than I am.
That would be doable.
I want to be better than I could ever be.
But I'm lost in my afterthoughts.
Who could change the world if there were still
dishes in the sink?
Who could write something great with an
unmade bed?
Why does the voice in my head call attention to
every little thing left undone?
Why is it never enough for something to be an
afterthought?

Food

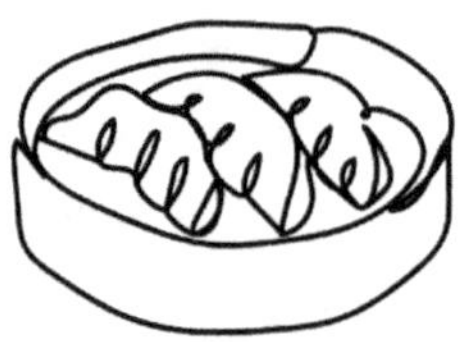

I don't like it when people watch me eat.
I don't know if it's because you told me I eat
like a savage or because he asked me if I had an
eating disorder after I passed out.
Funny how he never worried about an eating
disorder when he called me pudgy.
Or fat. Or talked about the effects of ranch on
my ass.
All I know is I eat quickly and in private to the
best of my ability because I don't want to talk
about it.
Or think about it.

Just a Trim

My hair is on the bathroom sink.
I needed to be different
And now I wish I never changed.

My hair is on the bathroom sink.
It stares at me in wonder.
Will it end up in the drain or the trash?

My hair is on the bathroom sink.
It used to be a threat.
They'd cut it if I didn't brush it daily.

My hair is on the bathroom sink.
A stranger's in the mirror.
I'm waiting for who I was to finally disappear,
But I'm not sure I'm ready for who I want to be.

Currents

I'm naked and all I can focus on is the dirt that builds up in my cracks and crevices as my body is dragged along the abandoned streets of the flooded town. There used to be people here. You'd see them in the shops without any doors buying things that don't seem to matter very much anymore. But that was then.

Now there's shallow flood water as I'm pulled through the wreckage of everything I took for granted. The life I never wanted, but always expected. The world I thought would always hold steady.

I'm being pulled away.

SECTION III

Ambition

I Do

You don't take me seriously, but I do.
I made my first business cards in the third grade.
I threw out the lipgloss to make a briefcase.
With eyeshadow residue.
You see my youthful ambitions and you laugh.
And I might have been just a weird little kid
But at the heart of everything that I did
Was pathetic eagerness.
When will you see that I'm not playing pretend?
Oh, why can't I just stop caring about you?
You don't take me seriously, but I do.

Canon

The LLCs and trademarks are in someone else's
name.
But I'm in love with what I see in someone
else's characters.
The chemistry the actors have is falling off the
screen.
The only problem that I see is that it isn't canon.
Can someone tell me that I'm not crazy?
That what I see is there?
That the person holding the pen is missing
something they themselves put there?

Admirable Lunatics

The master builder falls from the tower
The one she called him to create.
The destructive muse
The one who held him to every promise
The one who remembered every lie
Organia
A man will say anything to a foolish little girl if
he thinks he can get something from her
And he took something from her
And now she's taken something back

Siri

He wrote your story.
The noble woman brought low.
The evil lesbian.
The cheated, long suffering wife.
Every character a poor reflection of who you
must have been.
He didn't write of a woman who worked odd
jobs in the theater to support her kids.
Not the lady who left a comfortable life to create
her own art.
Those characters might outshine him.
You were The Stronger
On some level, he must have known that.

Aube

I'm staring out the window of the bunker that
I'm trapped in.
I know I could escape, but I'm a willing captive
Until I find a way to survive in this new world.
A world with rooms carved into hills and tiny
little fingers
All thoughts I have left in my head are written in
the mirror.
You can see it in my eyes.
I'm not satisfied,
But it's fine.

Prolific

It's never enough to write a scene.
One acts waste my time.
When I begin a task,
I do not aim at something minor.
If I am giving something my time,
It must be great.
At least to me.
And so I write full length plays.
Scene after scene.
Without ceasing.
Multiple drafts.
Writing. Rewriting.
Until my work lives up to my aims.

Outline

I don't know his name yet,
But I know his last line.
I think I know the feeling I want him to evoke at
the start.
I see the map of his story and how it folds into
hers and how they both belong in the set I
sketched, but not how they got there. Or what
they are to each other.
And it may show in time.
It's just an outline.

Archivist

You are your first archivist
Tell the story as you will
Burn the bitter letters
Destroy unwanted evidence.
Write down everything that matters.
Because when you die, others will come and
shove it all in boxes.
The story of your life will be in the basement of
a library.
Rarely visited.
A special collection.
But maybe one day you'll be someone's
micro-obsession.

A Modern Audience

Why did you change your painting?
Did it need to be more palatable?
Did you need to make it hurt less when your
father saw it?
Did you need your pain to be prettied up before
you could share it with the world?
Was the court case too personal and you had to
take something back?
How would you feel knowing we know what it
should've looked like?
Would you feel violated all over again or would
you finally feel seen?
Am I complicit in delving into the things you
never wanted to share or am I a part of seeing
the things you thought you had to hide?

Accomplished

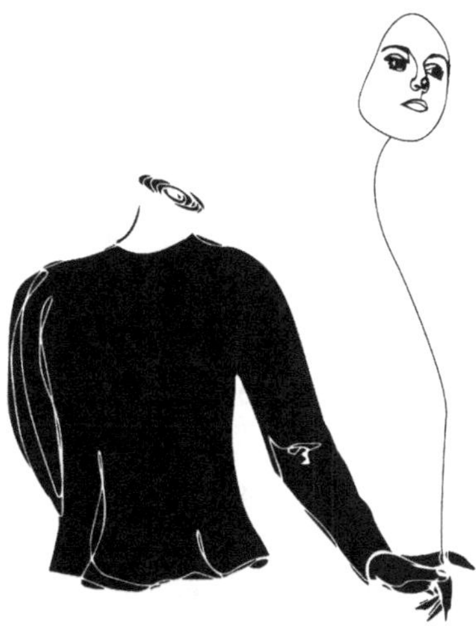

I sometimes wonder if I do the things I do because I want to do them or because I want others to be astounded.
Is my life just one long piece of performance art where I try to convince everyone that I'm special?
How long must I run from the failed expectations I project onto people that don't give a damn?
It's like I think that one day, one work, one piece will finally be enough for me to matter.
I can sing Zerlina's arias with a youthful whimsy.
I designed my own website at thirteen and it still works.

I was the captain of this and that club that
nobody cared about.
I wrote a full length play when I was nineteen.
And while it's clearly a reflection on the friends
I was so scorned by, there's a perfect scene just
waiting at the end–one that I cannibalized for
another play which would be my first
production.
I made the second highest position at my job in
less than a year after returning with my graduate
degree.
My thesis passed with flying colors in undergrad
and grad school.
Everything I put out, I get acclaim for the
unflinching emotional honesty that I can't give
to the people I love.
Because I'd rather hide behind my
accomplishments than let them see who I really
am.

Judy Darling

I want to break free from history.
To take things out of context.
To give things a new context.
One where they can live and learn and love
again.
To save you.
I remember when I found out how sad your life
was.
If you give a five-year-old a time machine.
But time went on, the same way it always does.

SECTION IV

Connection

Hopeless Soprano

I've been practicing my solo
For six weeks now.
You know she told me this morning
You let me down.
When I look to the audience
I see you there.
Now all the old lyrics are gone
Lost in your stare.
By the chorus, I've recovered.
I look away.
My coach asks me why I lost it
I give your name

Chicken Wire Crowns

I took the scraps of chicken wire and made them into crowns.
I make whimsy out of practical and wait to be let down.
The magic of Mary Poppins was snapping as you clean
The mundane becomes eventful if you let it be
But when I try to fly in clouds, I end up hitting earth.
I am no Mary Poppins, but I try. For what it's worth.
I wish I were an optimist with glasses all half full,
But every rosy glass I had was smashed with one dark look.

Inherited Trait

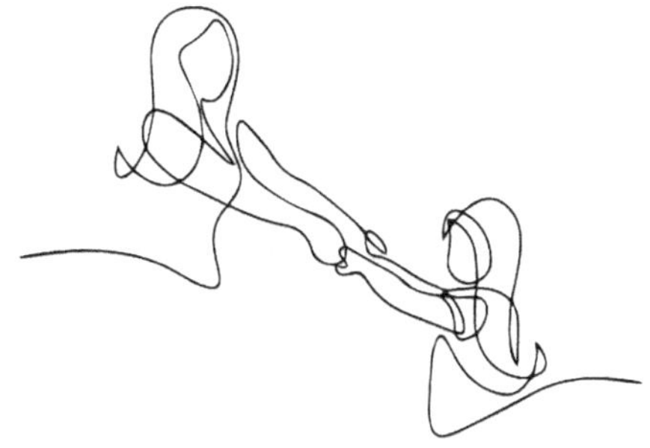

I think you wanted me to look like you
Or to get your eyes
Or your rosy-eyed world view
You probably wanted me to be a cheerleader like
you
Or a teacher like you
Or a mother like you
I'm a brown-eyed cynic with no rhythm, no
kids, and no teaching credentials.
But I'm stubborn like you.
Hardworking like you.
Resilient like you.
Those are my inherited traits.

Fighting the Giant's Ghost

It'd be easier for me if you were a smashing
success.
Or if you had lived to no acclaim in a quiet,
unremarkable life.
Instead you went down in a blaze of bad
decisions you couldn't charm your way out of.
And now it's not enough that I went further than
you in school. Or that I got a more stable job.
Or health care. Or a mortgage before thirty.
Because now I'm not competing with you.
I'm living in the shadow of the person you
might've been.
And he's grown into Goliath.

11:30 PM

It'd be nice to leave before midnight,
But there's always more to do.
Always another file to load.
Another invoice to send.
Another call to make.
What am I thinking? I can't call at this hour.
I'll schedule an email for 8:03 AM. That way it
doesn't seem scheduled, but it does make it
seem like they were top on my list of priorities.
I'm not even top of my list of priorities.
I dream of a day where I wake up, bolt out of
bed, and drive an hour to get fresh Krispy
Kreme before coming back to my condo to take
a bath. My condo doesn't have a bath, but this is
my dream. So I spend an hour or two in a
magically never-cooling bath before leaving to
walk through a nature preserve six states away.
It's 11:45 PM.
I still have work to do.

Swing

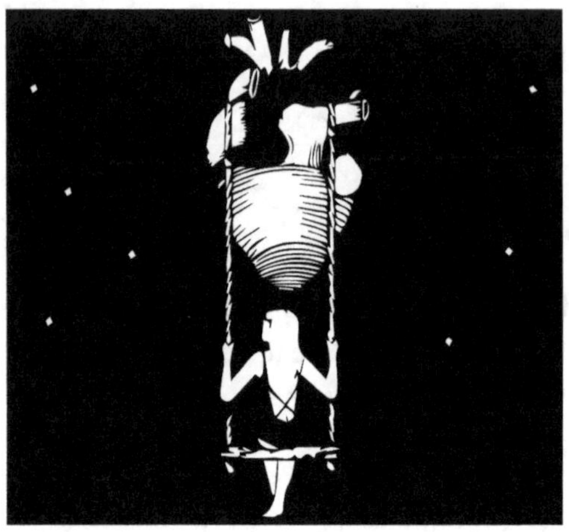

I'm sitting on the porch pushing back and forth
on my own.
I remember when you would push with me.
For me.
Before my legs were long enough to reach the
ground.
I remember the last time.
When you told me you wouldn't be around much
longer.
I remember that last talk.
The way your legs struggled to push us both.
The way I had to compensate.
I don't swing much anymore.

Rummikub

You're checking on my mental health.
It's why we play these games.
With all the best intentions, you make these little
plans,
But seem to think that I don't understand
Exactly what you're doing.
You want to check on me.
It's maintenance.
You're looking to see if I need new tires or an oil
change.
And I appreciate that you care, but sometimes I
just want someone to spend time with me
because they enjoy me.
At least I'm winning.

Thump

The thumps are so loud that I'm worried another tree has fallen.
So I leave my room.
Before I can make it to the yard, I run into you banging your head against the cabinets where we keep the glasses and the Yugioh plate we used to fight over.
And now you're only fighting with yourself.
I run up and hold you because I hate being touched, but I love you.
And I can't watch you do this.
You stop with the banging because you don't want to hurt me.
You only want to hurt yourself.
I wish I knew how to help you.

Paris Gellar

People see me as intimidating.
They always have.
Teachers tell me to sit out in group projects
because I overwhelm others.
I have conversations and people feel off-kilter. I
guess I'm too direct.
It's just how I am.
And now I bake cookies and give in and do
everything I can to be approachable.
Once in a while it works.

A Ghost of Fandoms Past

I know inside jokes a deep, deep lore that'll
never take me anywhere.
I'm embarrassed of things I posted on alt
accounts.
I'm struggling to accept how obsessed I was.
And your videos still make me laugh, but I'll
leave the conspiracies alone, thanks.
Maybe it was easier to lose myself into someone
else's life before I understood boundaries.
Maybe it was easier to throw myself headfirst
into love when I had the comfortable distance of
knowing I'd never actually know you.
Is it wrong that I miss how intense it all was?
Like, I'm sure the fans must scare you, but on
our side there's this faux connection and, while
you believe it, it's wonderful.
Getting to devote yourself to something.

Three AM

I'm sitting on the bathroom counter as you bathe
Listening to every crisis we won't remember
next month as I paint my toes a cherry red
I long for these meaningless conversations
I miss holding you as you cried against the tile
floor.
I miss dancing with you in the kitchen.
I miss sleeping next to you at night.
Most of the time I can ignore it.
But not at three AM.

DVD Commentary

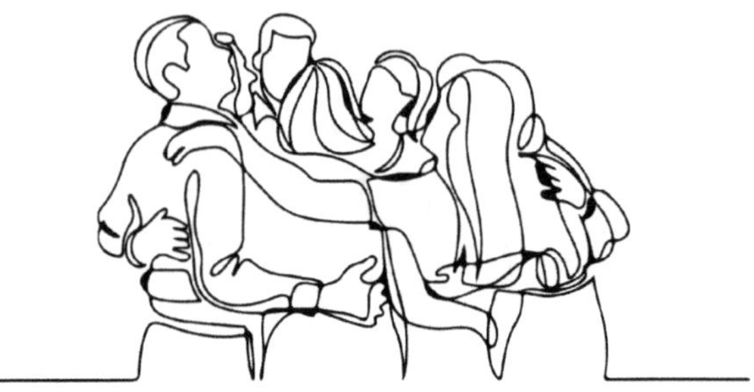

There are stories only we can tell
Because we're the ones that lived it.
They may see the finished project,
But they'll never know what went into it.
You're the only thing I know this fucking well.
But the you I know is in 2012
And I'm a stranger here.
I made a table for your wedding and a bookshelf
for your baby shower.
But I don't know you now.
Everything we built, every bond we shared–
Everything is caught behind this distance.
Do you remember holding me in the parking lot
at church as I broke down?
Do you remember being vampires and
werewolves?
How do you remember it now?

Because my memories are of someone who used
to really care, but let me go a million times
before I walked away.
And if I don't text back this time,
I'm not upset. I swear.
I just can't.
Because talking over Breakfast Club was sacred
to me then,
But now I value peace of mind.
And you can't give me that.

House Call

I can hear tears in your voice.
You didn't call to catch up
Or to see if I finally left work.
Someone said something and now, you're
spiraling.
And I'm listening and caring in the moment,
But after I realize how beautiful it is that you
call me when you spiral.
And it helps me to know that I'm not the only
one spiraling in all of this uncertainty as life gets
more and more complicated.

I'mnothangingupI'mnothangingupI'mnothangin
gupI'mnothangingupI'mnothangingupI'mnothangingu
pI'mnothangingupI'mnothangingupI'mnothangingupI'mnoth
angingupI'mnothangingupI'mnothangingupI'mnothangingupI'mnoth
angingupI'mnothangingupI'mnothangingupI'mnothangingupI'mnothangingupI'
mnothangingupI'mnothangingupI'mnothangingupI'mnothangingupI'mnothangingupI'mnothang
ingupI'mnothangingupI'mnothangingupI'mnothangingupI'mnothangingupI'mnothangingupI'mnothangingupI'mnothan
gingupI'mnothangingupI'mnothangingupI'mnothangingupI'mnothangingupI'mnothangingupI'mnothangingupI'mnothangingupI'mnothang
ingupI'mnothangingupI'mnothangingupI'mnothangingupI'mnothangingup

SECTION V

Intended

One of Your Kind

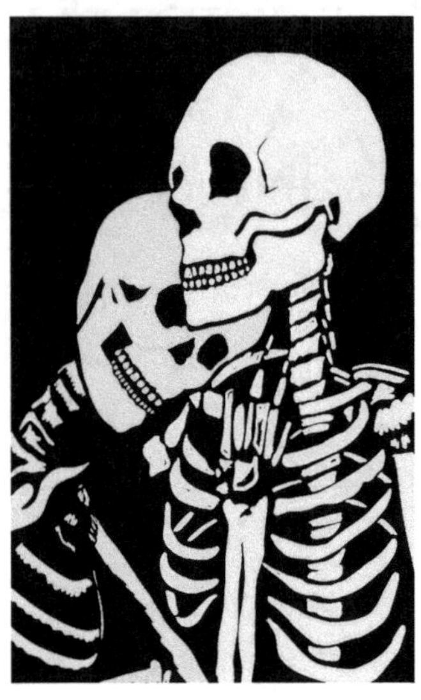

Charcoal stains your fingers
Black's smudged around your eyes
You're every adolescent fantasy
I knew I had to hide
Your laundry smells like springtime
I washed yours with mine
Your eyes, they promise trouble
I pretend I'm not the kind
The kind that welcomes trouble as it tears into
her flesh
The kind who opens gladly to your violent
caress

The kind who planned our future before I even
knew your name
The kind who's kind of desperate that you will
feel the same
I'm not the kind I thought I was before
The only kind I am is yours

Paris When it Sizzles

I dream of Audrey Hepburn leaning over me
Talking about her studies in depravity
Laughing with me as I write.
I don't want a muse, but I want someone who
cares what I'm writing.
Who cares if I ate at all today.
Who cares if I slept at all last night.
And if they undo their hair while I drink a Dr.
Pepper on the rocks, that'd be nice.

Butterflies

The stage is empty except for me
And the only thing I want is for you to notice
Every note to every song is meant to lull you
into complacency
So you won't replace me
I'll walk the tightrope juggling axes if it means
you won't look away.

Nightmare

There's a reason I ghost you.
The reason is you.
It's the football game after we broke up where
you told everyone I was curvy, ran your hand
down my body, and told me you loved me as I
ran away feeling violated.
It's the love letters you sent her long after she
told you to stop.
It's the fact that you weren't just my first kiss,
but hers.
She was two years younger than me,
I was two years younger than you.
She was in fucking middle school.
It's finding out all these ugly things I didn't
know.

It's reanalyzing all the little moments where I
gave you the benefit of the doubt.
And now the only time I think of you is in my
nightmares.

Comfort

You were never a perfect person,
But I treasure your memory
Because for one sweet moment you held as I
broke in two.
So if you slept through our last date, it's fine.
If you moved on too quickly, it's alright.
Because when I needed you most,
You were by my side
And I'll never forget that.

The Exception

I've never been one for blondes,
But somehow you pull it off.
Physical contact freaks me out,
But you resting your head in my lap is just fine.
I can't deal with paragraph texts,
But you can write me a novel–it's fine.
You're the exception to every rule.

Something

Your hands dwarf mine
Each callus reminds me of a half-ass project I
begged you not to start
Your grip is too strong and too steady because
you hold everything painfully tight–as if I'll be
snatched away
I've given up on lotion; I'm moisturized by the
sweat of your palms
You call me unromantic because I'd sooner lift
you above my head than walk hand-in-hand on a
Sunday stroll
I may not want to hold your hand, but I want to
share your life.
That's gotta count for something.

Cancer

You met me in the time where I started talking
all about my star sign.
You were a cancer.
I didn't quite know what that meant, all I knew
was an aquarius should dress cute
And whatever was on my CoStar.
Then you started buying me lunch to make sure I
ate and I loved that,
But my independent nature meant I fought you
the whole way.
But you wouldn't stop trying.
And that unnerved me.

It was charming that you wanted to take care of
me.
It was startling that you didn't listen when I told
you no.

Because even if my boundaries are stupid, they
are mine.
But I said 'It's fine.
Just please don't do it again.
I mean it.'

And we just kept on that way.
I was not-so-silently bothered by you always
ignoring every word I'd say.
But it became routine.
And I just stopped fighting.
After all, it was nice,
In a controlling way.
Maybe my aquarius sun was pushing me to push
you away, so I tried to ignore it.
But you were a cancer.

So so much more happened.
I told you I didn't want you to touch me,
I didn't want anyone to touch me.
It's just one of my things.
But you kept putting your hand on my back.
How many times did I ask you not to do that?
I can't count them.

And you'd tell me I was a terrible friend,
Then invite me to the movies.
I thought it was you making amends;
A way to say it wouldn't happen again.

I watched the movie and you grabbed my hand.
I wrote it off as you needing comfort.
After all, it was a scary movie.
It's just a little thing.
But the little things were growing larger still.

One night you asked to come with me to the
practice rooms.
That was the first time you heard me sing.
You said I amazed you.
It lit me up as my voice is my greatest insecurity.
But I amazed you.
And then you followed me home.
I told you not to.
I tried to write it off as you being too nice
because, after all, a girl walking home at that
hour is the start of a new story.
But it made me uncomfortable.
I was never scared of walking alone in the dark,
Until you became my shadow.

When I broke down crying because of a man I
had trusted making headlines for his own
misdeeds, Molly ran interference telling you that
you weren't what I needed.
And I thanked her.
And you stormed away.

The next day you showed me a video on youtube
and when I didn't laugh in the first minute, you
slammed it closed.
And then you spent fifteen minutes apologizing
for making things uncomfortable.
And you made me comfort you.
Because kids in school were mean.
Because life was really hard.
Because you were sensitive.
I didn't want to break you apart
With my honesty.
But honestly.
You were a cancer.

To Know You

I want the words that you can't say.
The silence in your speech.
I want the far off place you go
Always out of reach.
I want the thoughts you're scared to think.
The guilt that's in your stare.
I want to know the secret things
That only you can share.
I want to hold you through the night.
And know what keeps you up.
Feel the tears you're scared to cry
Falling on my shirt

Lancelot

I like when you defend me
And when you back me up
I like the plans we make
And every sweet shared look
I like the way I'm feeling
Your hands inside my hair
I like the way you saved me
By showing me you care

Question Mark

Life was simple.

Periods. Exclamation marks! Maybe an occasional dash-

And then I met a question mark.

They walked in and suddenly everything was different.

The sky was green and I spoke French.

And now I'm questioning everything.

Pink Moon

There's something different about tonight.
Sitting on the front porch late as the cicadas are
playing our song.
We're waiting for the world to turn upside down.
The moon is pink and we're walking on our
hands around the pool that just appeared.
I hope we don't slip.
I remember when things made sense.
But the moon is pink, I've had three hours of
sleep, and the only thing I've eaten today is a
chicken biscuit.

SECTION VI

Alienation

Husk

A half pound of shrimp over a bed of peppers
and onions
A plate of pasta with chicken and cheese
A twelve-layer cake with a scoop of ice cream
And you're still empty.
Every light is on.
All the plugs are in.
Nothing has been powered down.
And you're still empty.
I've given you every hour I had
My eyes, my ears, my heart
I've been consumed.
And you're still empty.
The void inside you is a quicksand that
swallowed me little by little from which I could
never escape.

Tire Marks

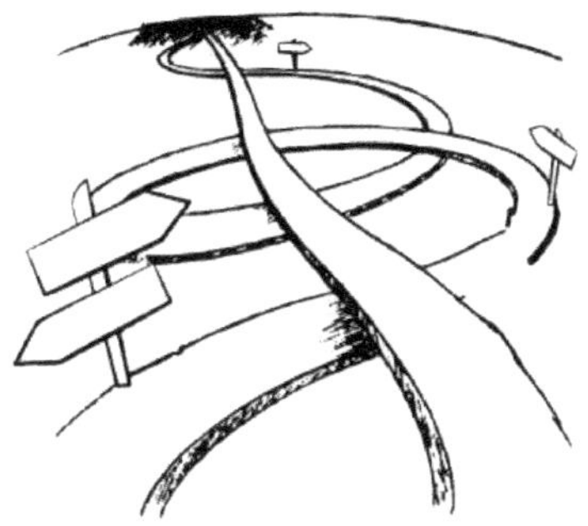

Leaving was always an escape
It was the way out
The way I could find a better place
One where I felt comfortable
Accepted
Loved
But I always wanted to stay
I wanted to believe I could make things change
Right where I was
Make a way to be comfortable
Accepted
Loved
Right where I was.
I'm leaving a trail of tire marks.

Linger

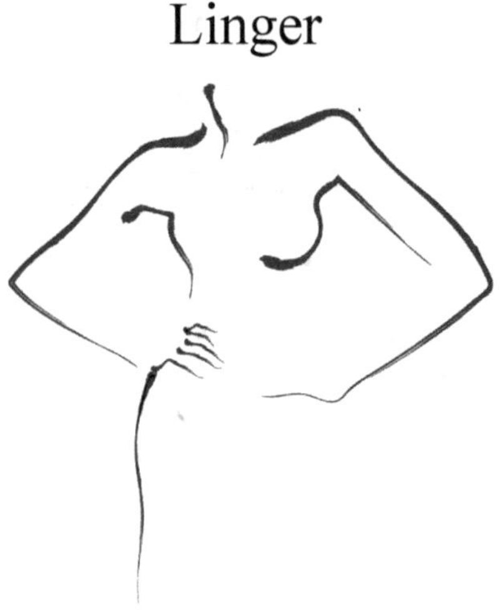

A hand on my back
    As you move behind my desk
        to throw something away.
There are other trash cans
    You chose the only one that
        lets you invade my space.
And I set no boundaries

Because it's easier to tell myself it's just the
trash.
    It's just a hand on my back.
        Nothing more.
    It's just a hand on my back.
        Nothing more.
    It's just a hand on my back.
        Nothing more.

It's just a hand on my back. Nothing more.
It's just a hand on my back.
Nothing more.
It's just a hand on my back.
Nothing more.
It's just a hand on my back. Nothing more.
But my hair still stands on end.

Crew Work

We're in the corner
Hidden from view
We wear all black
And try not to peak threw
The red curtains.
We light the lights
And we press the suits.
Wearing our headphones
And whispering cues
To the performers.
If you ever wonder why the actors put their
hands to front and back after their bows,
That would be us.
The little people doing unseen work.

Sanctuary

Hiding in the shadows on the backsteps
Praying you won't find me
And you do.
I wish I felt safe here.
Kids can be so mean.
Showing up on Sunday in my Easter dress
Praying you won't see me
And you do.
Kids can be so mean,
But they're not the problem.
You are.

Man, you're in your forties fighting with a
seventeen-year-old girl.
Because your testimony doesn't move me.
Not when I've seen your daughter crying on the
floor. Scared that you're coming home.
Finding God is wonderful, but it doesn't erase
who you were to her.
And I saw the way you used her belief to
manipulate.
If you want to make me out to be the big bad
wolf, that won't intimidate.
Because a man who picks a fight with a teenager
is not a man.
He's a wolf in sheep's clothing.

Is it still funny to you?

I remember how funny you thought it was when
you grabbed my chest and I screamed.
You're just a girl. I shouldn't be upset.
I remember how you used to unzip my dress or
bite at my hips as I stood up from the church
van.
It's funny because of my reaction.
My reaction is that you need to keep your teeth
to yourself. I'm not yours to consume
Because my body isn't only mine if it's a man
that wants to violate me.
And two girls groping each other isn't a joke.

It's especially not a joke if one of them's
screaming no.
I don't know if I was a barbie doll for you as you
explored your youth.
But I do know I feel uncomfortable when
anyone touches me.
And I think it's because of you.

Boxed In

I'm hiding in box office with the safes and the
candy hoping you won't come back.
You're drunk again and taking the opportunity to
curse out any woman in sight.
I wish I didn't find you terrifying.
I wish I was an action star that punched every
misogynist in the face.
But I don't want to be the kind to hurt others.
Revenge wouldn't sink me to your level.
But it'd take me lower than I am now.

Shaping

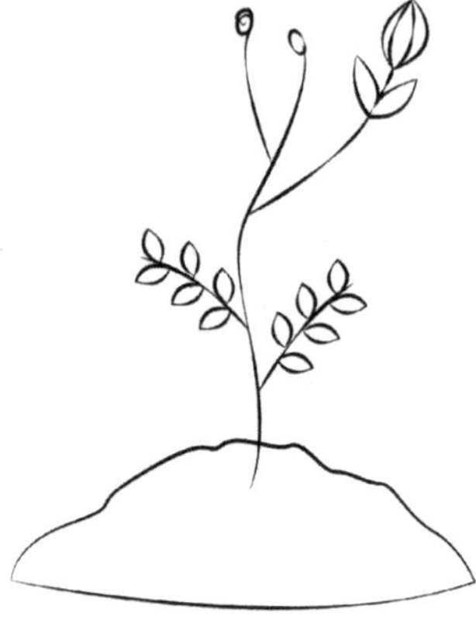

I still remember that day.
I was at your house.
Why was I at your house?
And you dropped something.
I bent down to grab it, and when I stood back up
you told me I needed to shave.
I haven't heard from you in ten years.
I think you moved. You must be in your forties
now.
I'm different now.
I'm not fifteen; sixteen; seventeen; eighteen.
I don't bend.
I shave daily.
I date guys a year or two younger.
Never older.

The Voice Change

In customer service, it's a high register.
Living in my head with a bell canto cadence and
handing back change as I wish you a good show.
In a commanding role, it's a deep chest voice as
if belting out orders will make someone take me
seriously.
With friends and family, it's a mixed register
taking what I need from what I have to fill
whatever it is they need from me at the time.
On a stage, it's espressivo because when you're
performing you're allowed to feel.

I let my heart out for people to see that under the
jokes and the snark is a creature that actually
cares–hoping they won't laugh at her.
In my house, it's a rest between measures.
Living in the silence allows me time to live
between the different versions of me.

Coded

I listen to the Smiths.
I dance in the rain.
I mirror the ID you wish you could follow.
I dress wildly.
And I teach you a lesson in the end.
Because I'm a fairytale creature to you.
I can only be broken if it's relatable.
I can only act out if it's entertaining.
I live on the back burner waiting for you to need
me again.
And you will.

Not for You

I'm kind of glad you slapped my hand,
Because it made me realize something very
important about myself.
Before you did that, I thought I did everything
for you.
I work my ass off everyday.
I do everything I can find to do.
I make everything around here work,
But I don't do it for you.
You benefit from my insanity,
But I do it because I wanted everything I do to
be incredible.
And if I'm a part of you, you're going to be
incredible.
Even if I have to drag it out of you.

Missed Communication

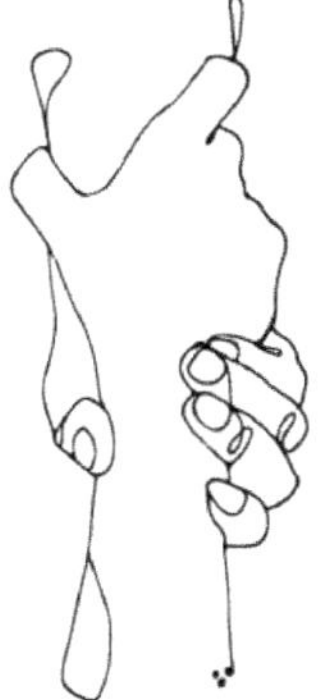

We talk around the things that we don't say.
I build fences around the things you don't want
me to bring up and try not to cross those lines
again.
I always cross that line again.
Because sometimes things come up that are
more important than what makes you
comfortable.
Sometimes I need you to tell me where the
boundaries are and why.
Because the fences are turning into gates that
boxes me into a space so small I have to fold
myself up to fit into it and I'm not one for yoga,
so I can't contort
And then I cross a line I didn't see and cut
myself in half as your obvious displeasure
sweeps over me.
I can't live like this.